TO:

_____

FROM:

_____

I NEED ALL THE FRIENDS I CAN GET

BY

CHARLES M. SCHULZ

PENGUIN WORKSHOP
An imprint of Penguin Random House LLC

This edition published by Penguin Workshop, an imprint of Penguin Random House LLC, New York, 2022

PEANUTS and all related titles, logos and characters are trademarks of Peanuts Worldwide LLC

© 1964 Peanuts Worldwide LLC. Originally published 1964.

Penguin supports copyright. Copyright fuels creativity, encourages diverse voices,
promotes free speech, and creates a vibrant culture. Thank you for buying an authorized edition
of this book and for complying with copyright laws by not reproducing, scanning, or distributing
any part of it in any form without permission. You are supporting writers and allowing
Penguin to continue to publish books for every reader.

PENGUIN is a registered trademark and PENGUIN WORKSHOP is a trademark of Penguin Books Ltd, and
the W colophon is a registered trademark of Penguin Random House LLC.

Visit us online at penguinrandomhouse.com.

Library of Congress Cataloging-in-Publication Data is available.

Manufactured in China

ISBN 9780593519677   10 9 8 7 6 5 4 3 2 TOPL

I NEED ALL THE FRIENDS I CAN GET

"Well,
I hate
to spoil all
the fun, but I
have to be
going."

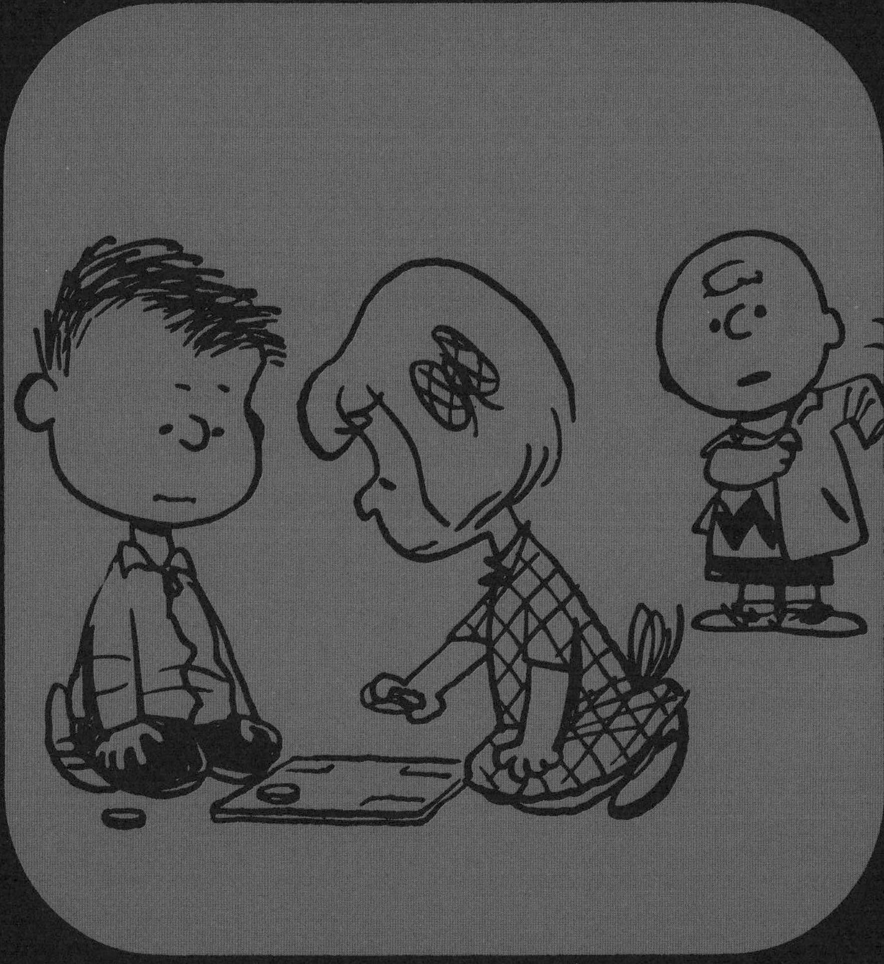

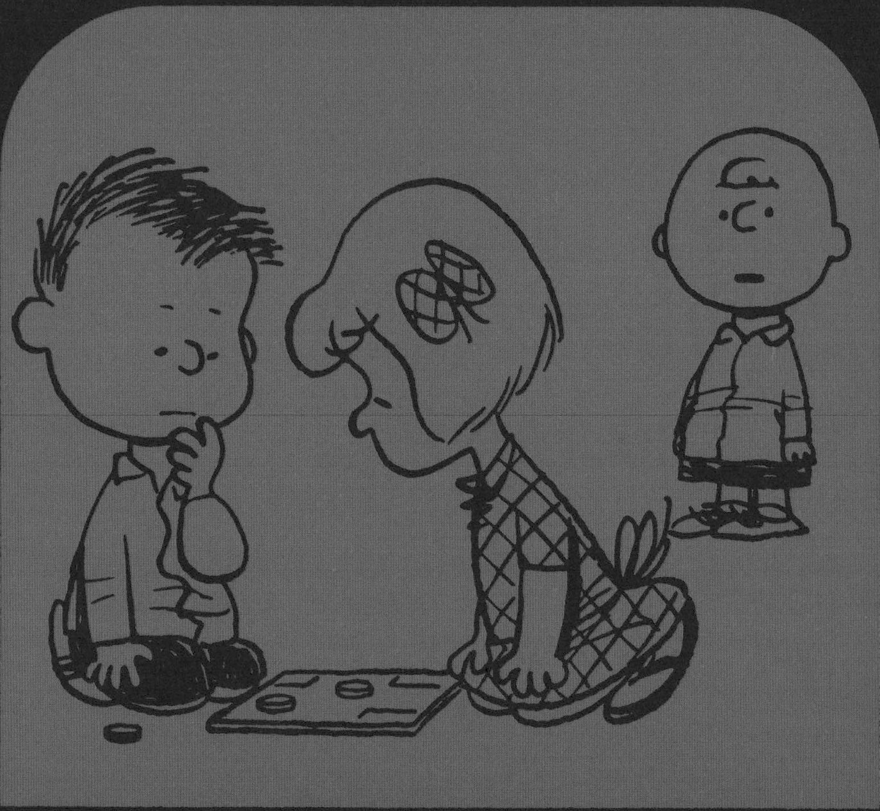

‘I said, I hate to spoil all the fun, but I have to be going.”

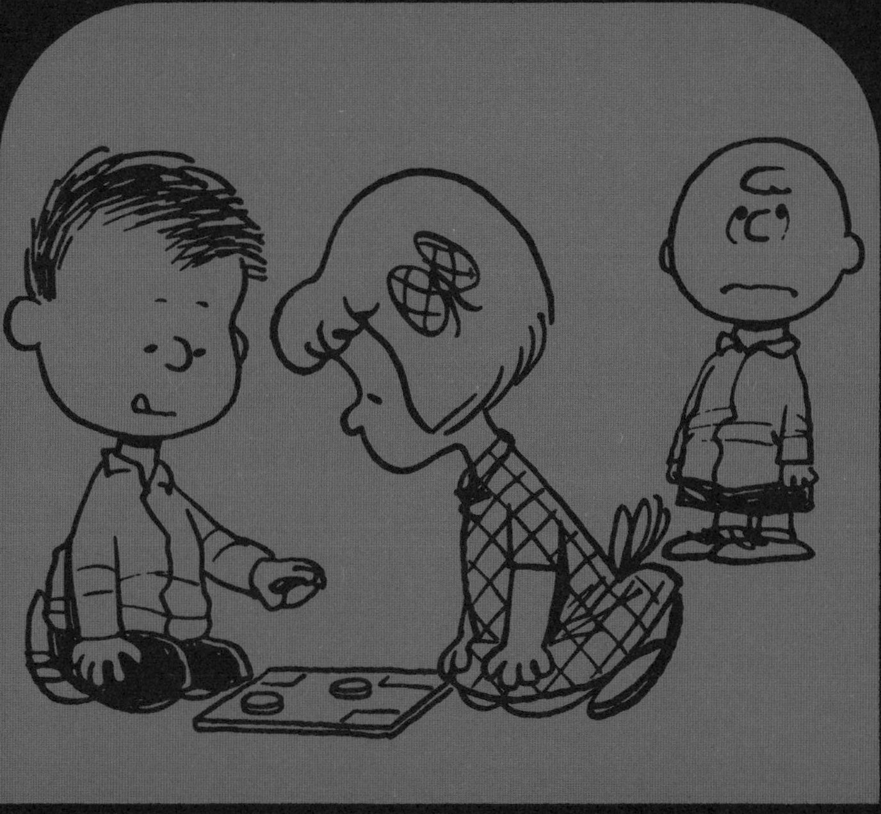

“Sigh!”

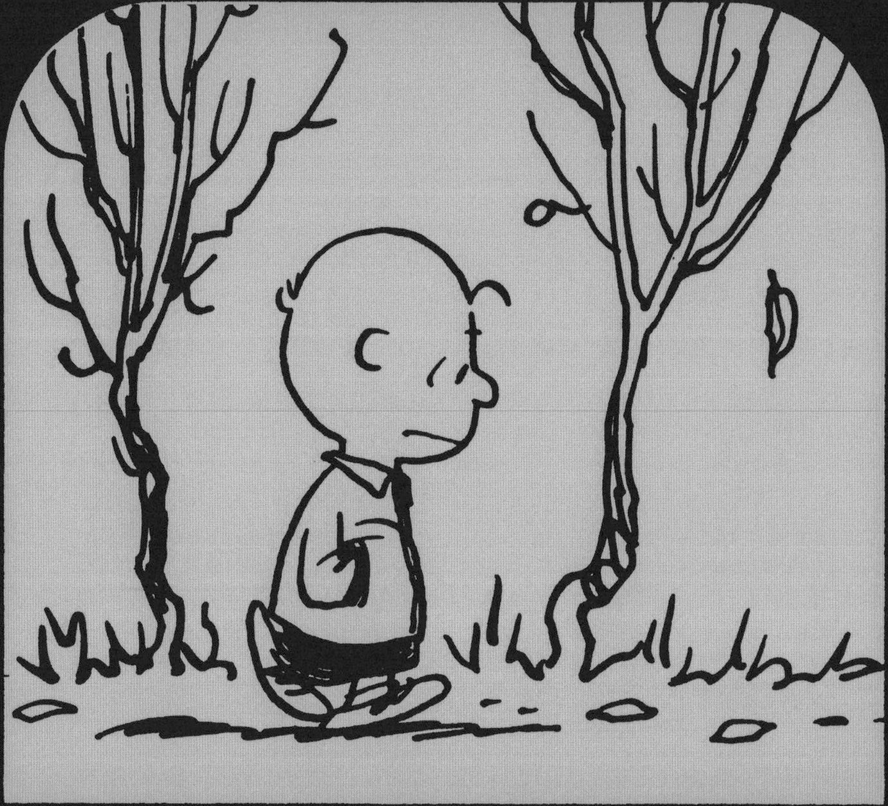

"Nobody likes me . . .
Nobody cares if I live or die!"

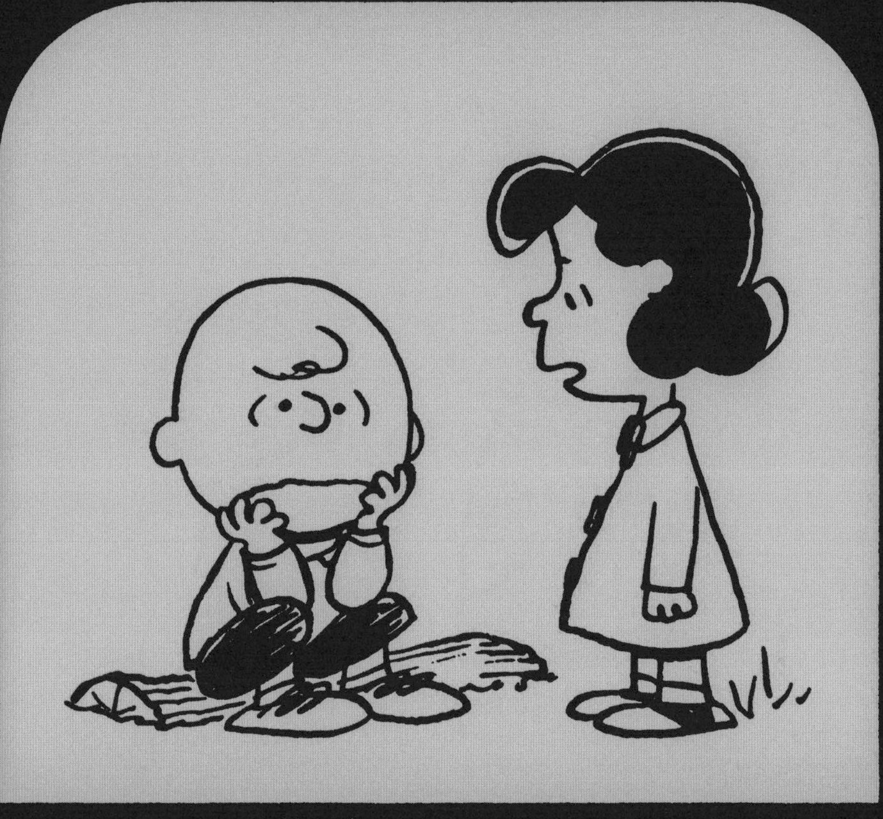

‘What’s the matter with you?”

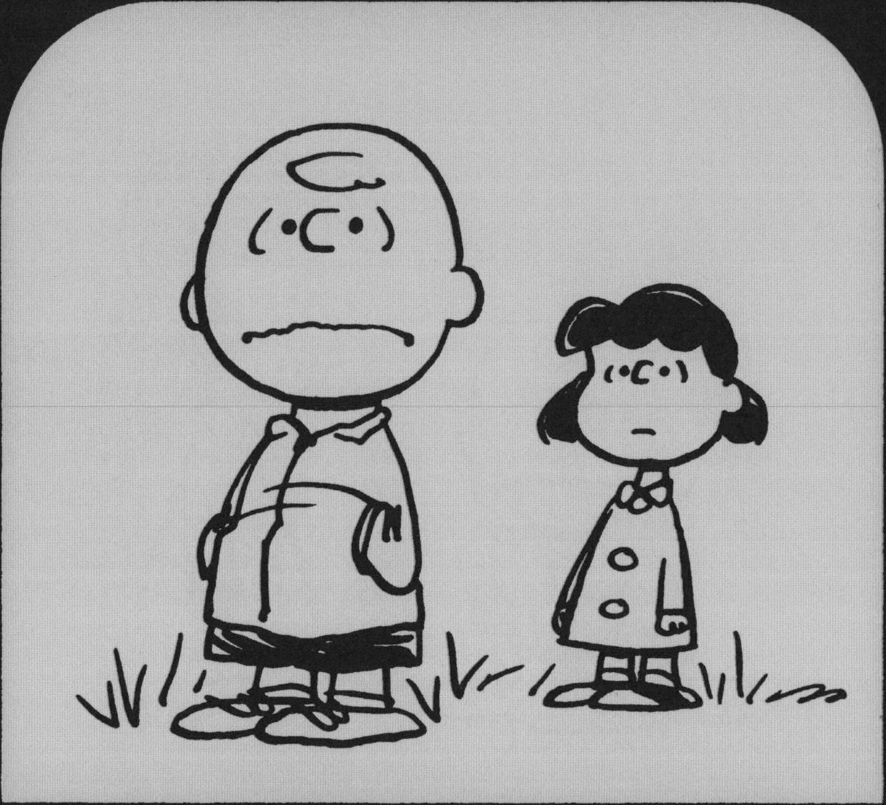

"I don't have any friends . . . I don't have one single person I can call a friend."

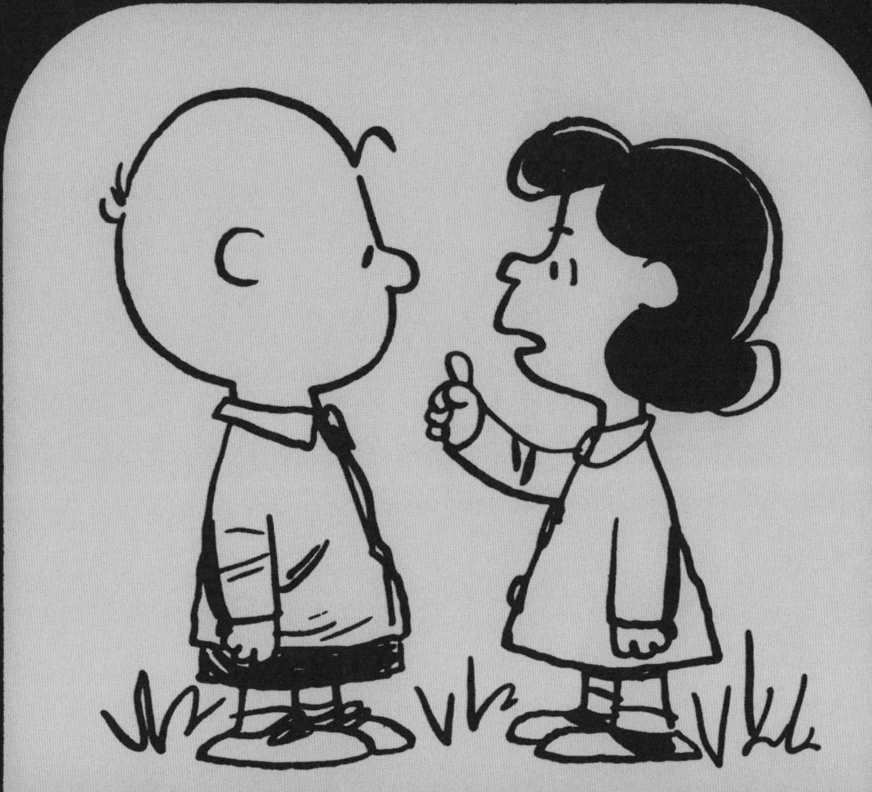

"Define 'Friend'!"

"A friend is someone you can sock on the arm!"

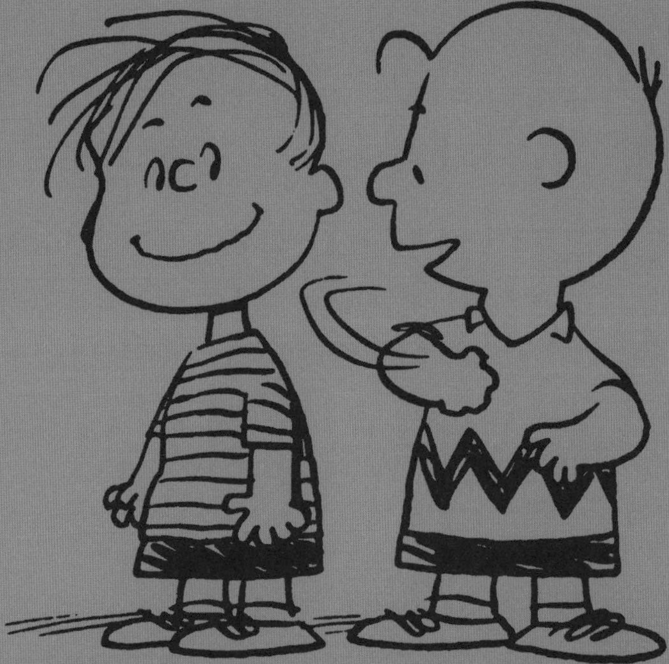

"A friend is someone who will take the side with the sun in his eyes."

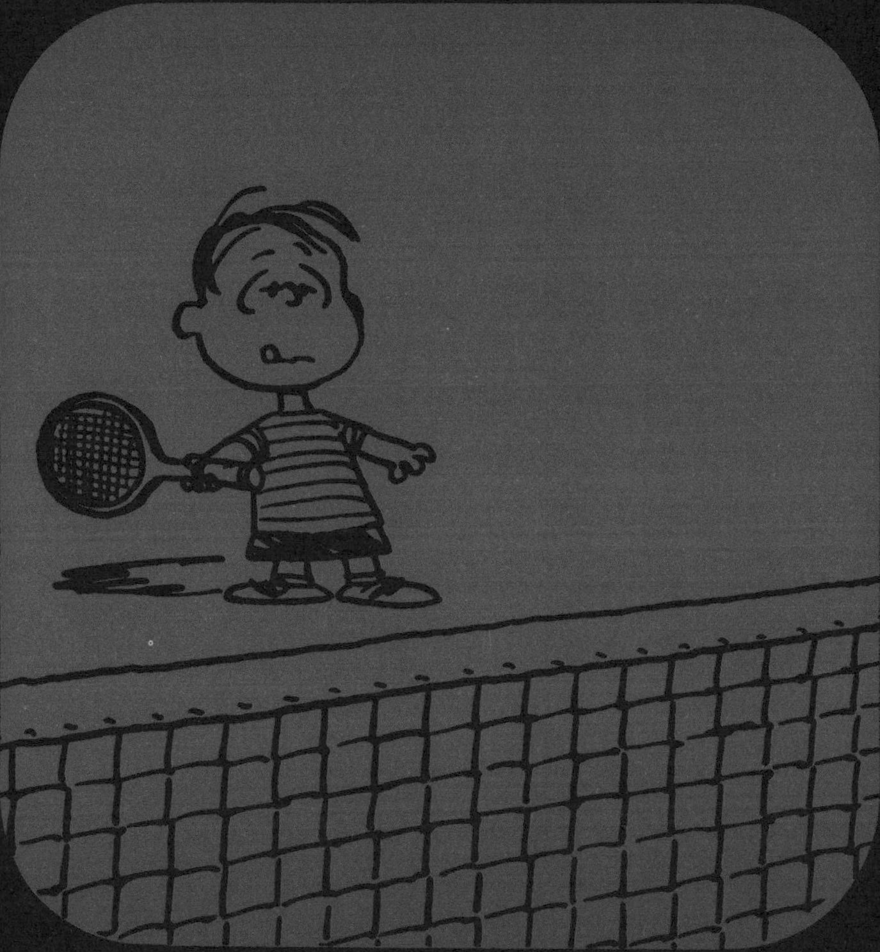

"A friend
is someone
who's willing to
watch the program
you want to
watch!"

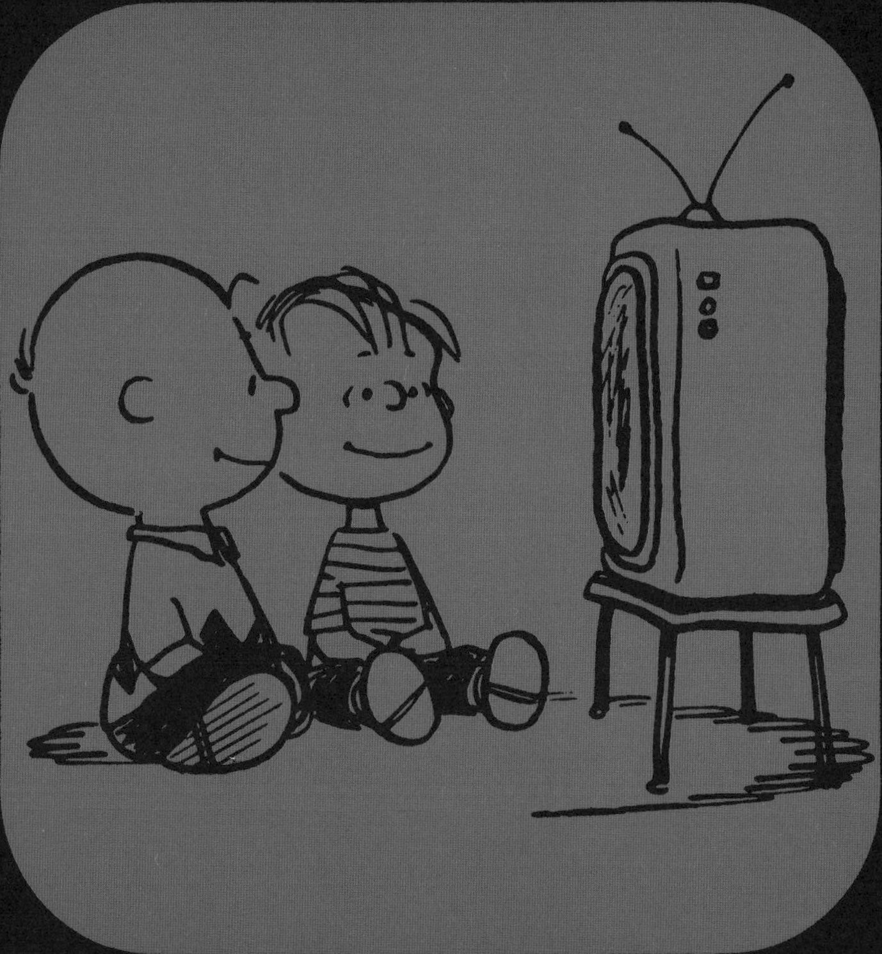

"A friend is someone who likes you even when the other guys are around."

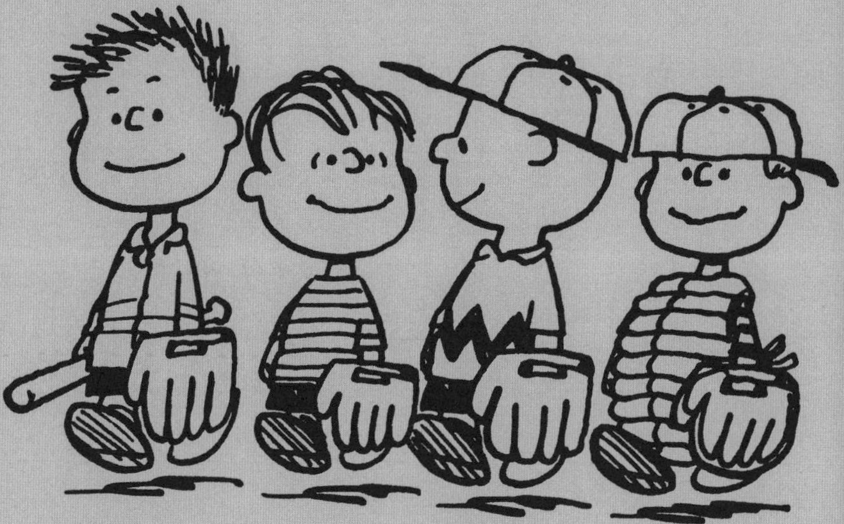

"A friend is someone who will share his home with you."

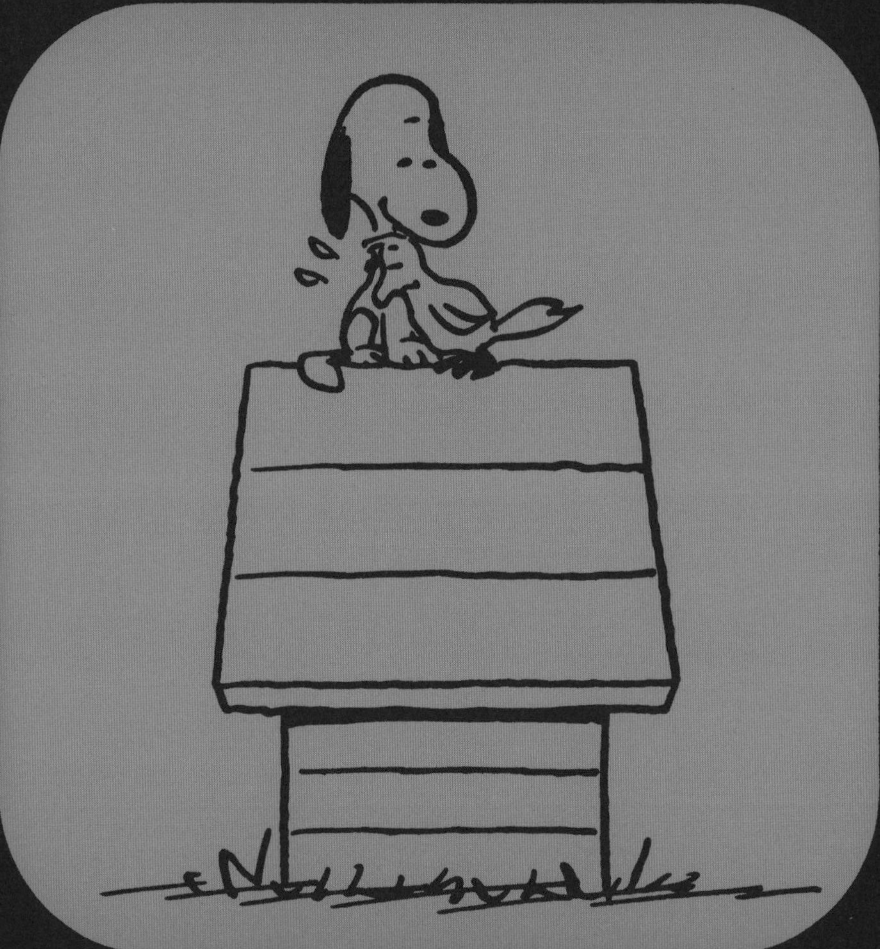

"A friend is someone who will trade you an Alvin Dark for a Luis Aparicio."

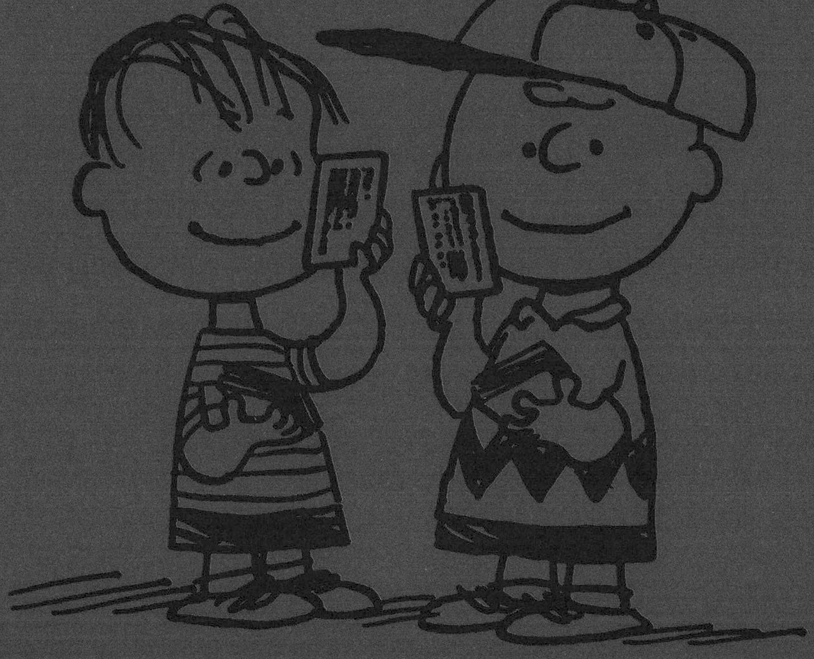

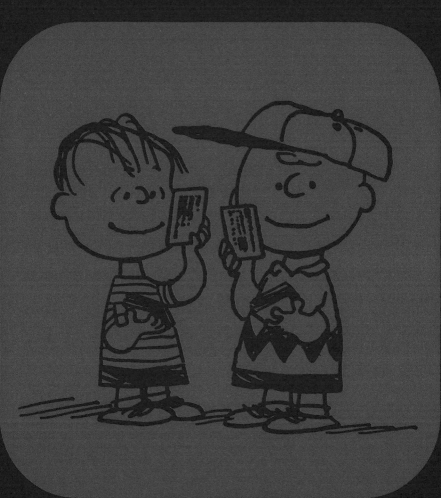

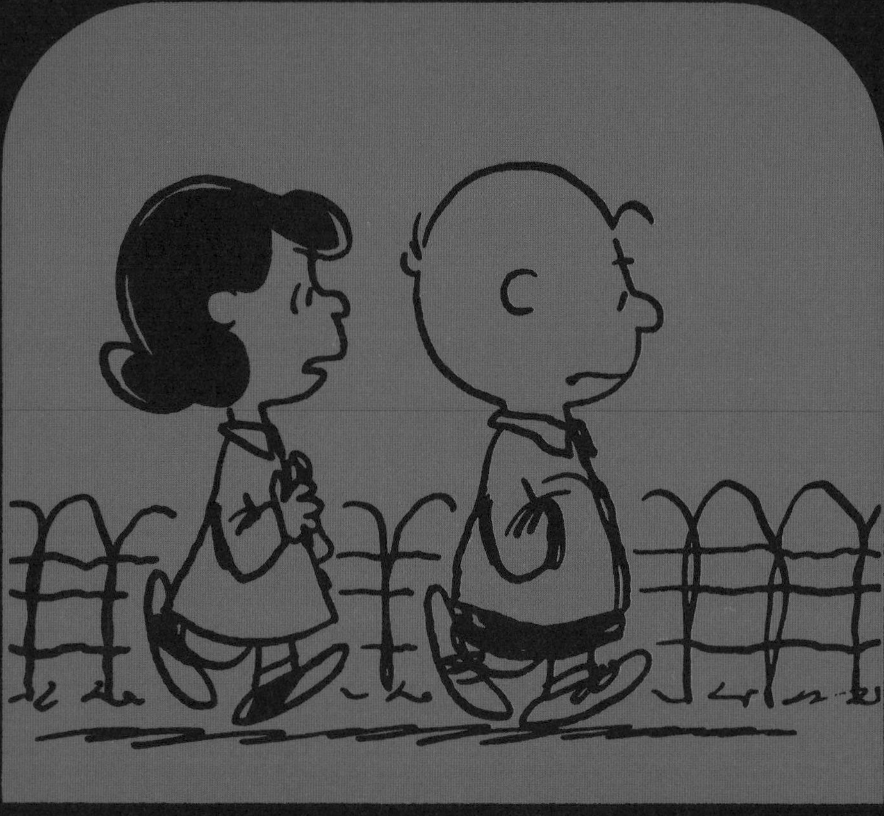

"I think you try too hard, Charlie Brown . . .
Be like me. I don't need any friends . . .
I'm self-sufficient!"

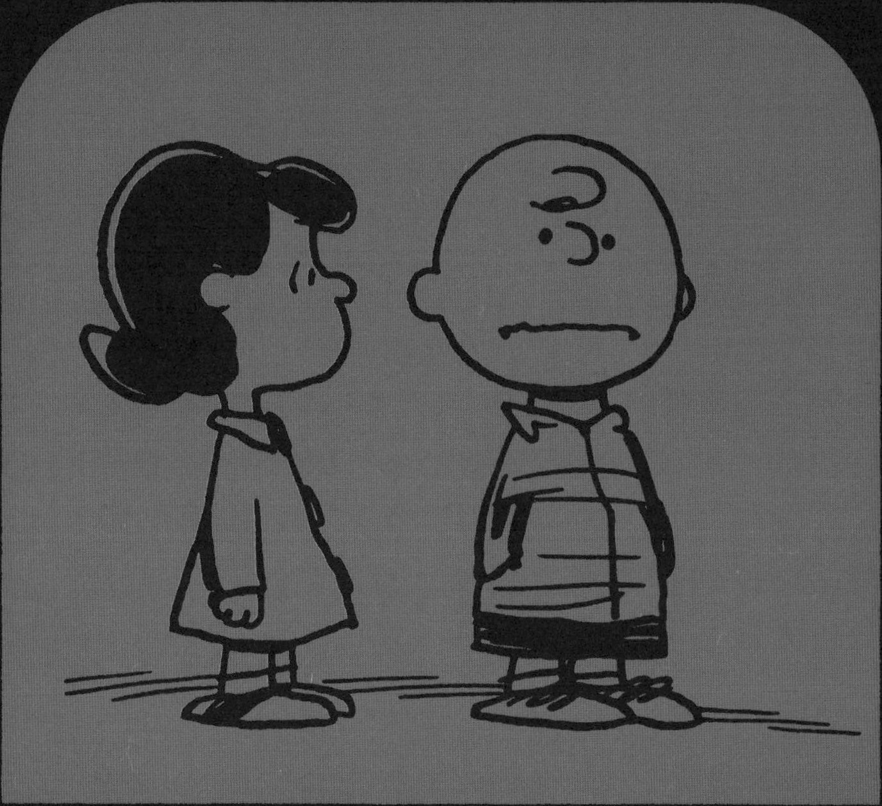

"Not me . . . I need
all the friends I can get!"

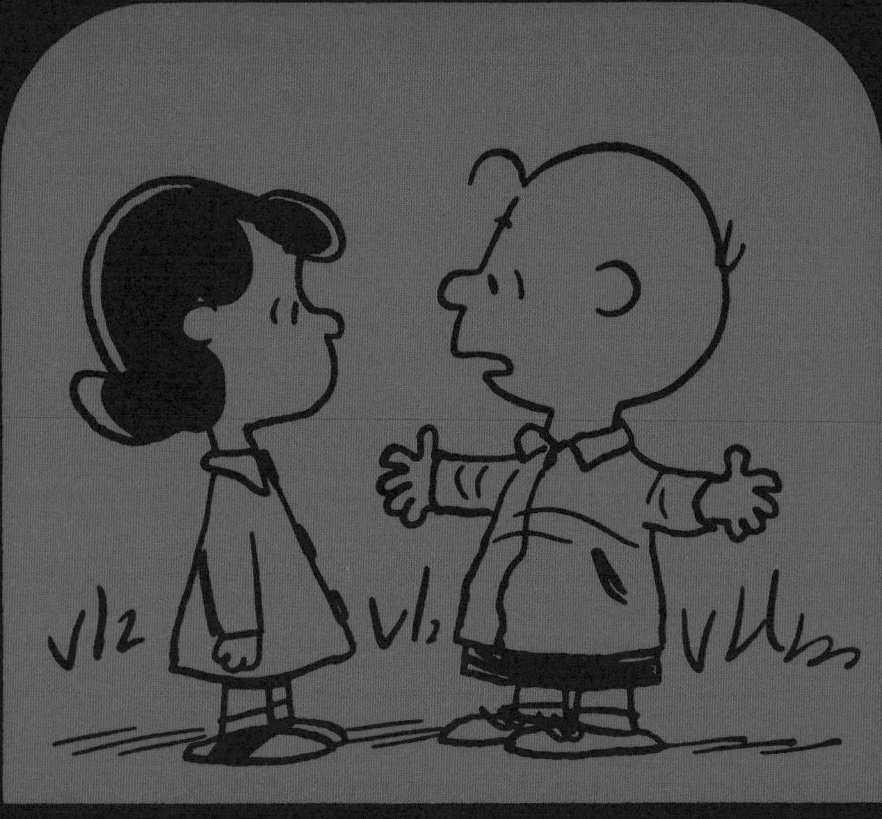

"I'd even settle for
a 'fair-weather' friend!"

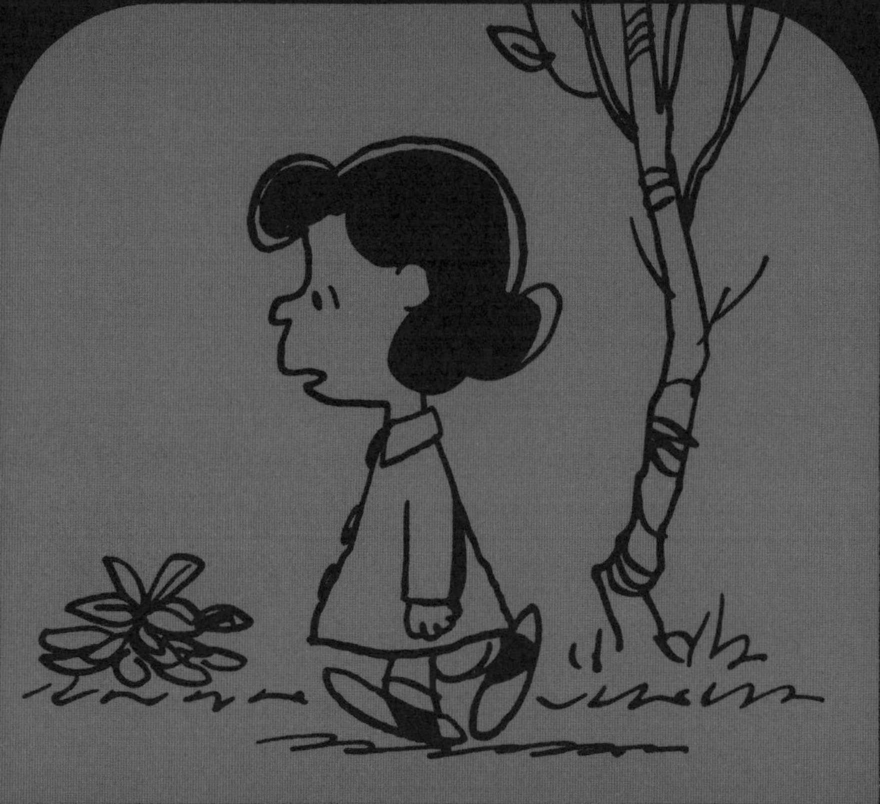

"Poor ol' Charlie Brown . . .
He really should try to be like me.
don't care if I have any friends or not . . .

"Just so
I'm popular!"

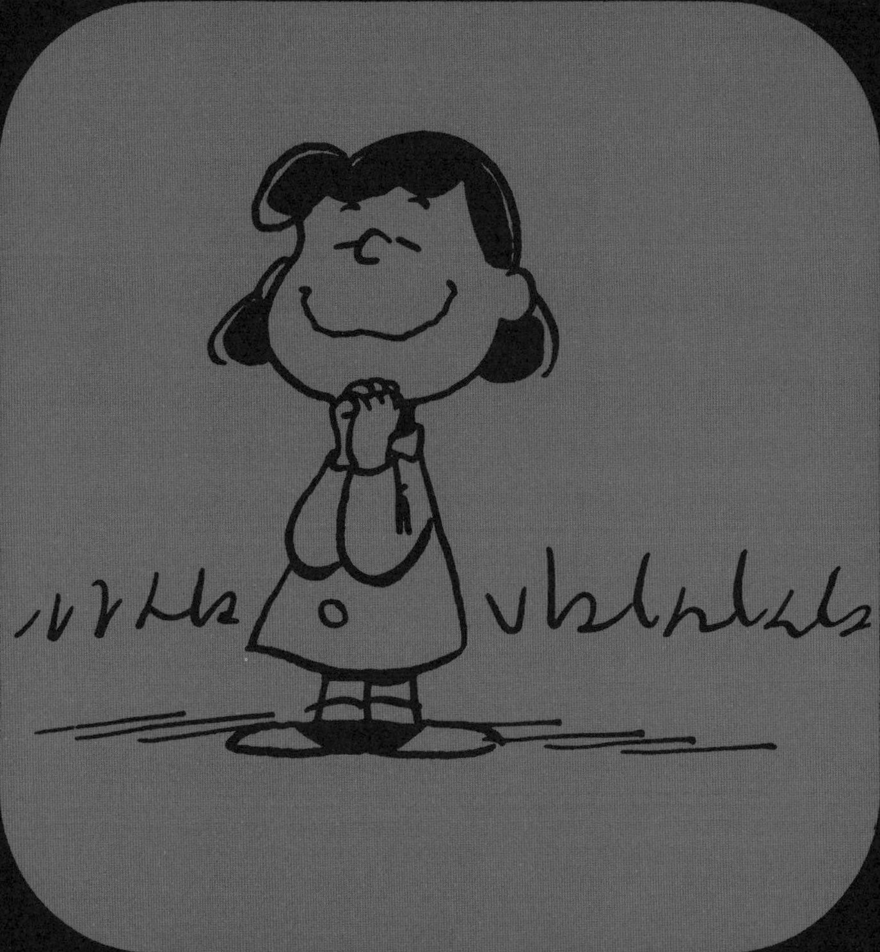

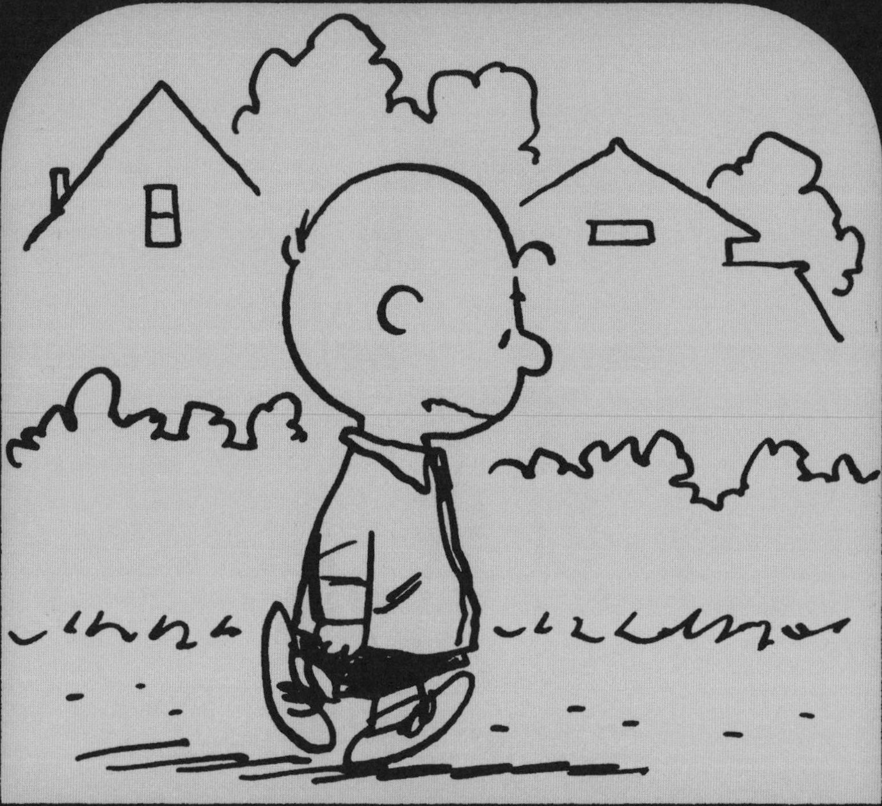

"I don't know...Talking to her never does much for me..."

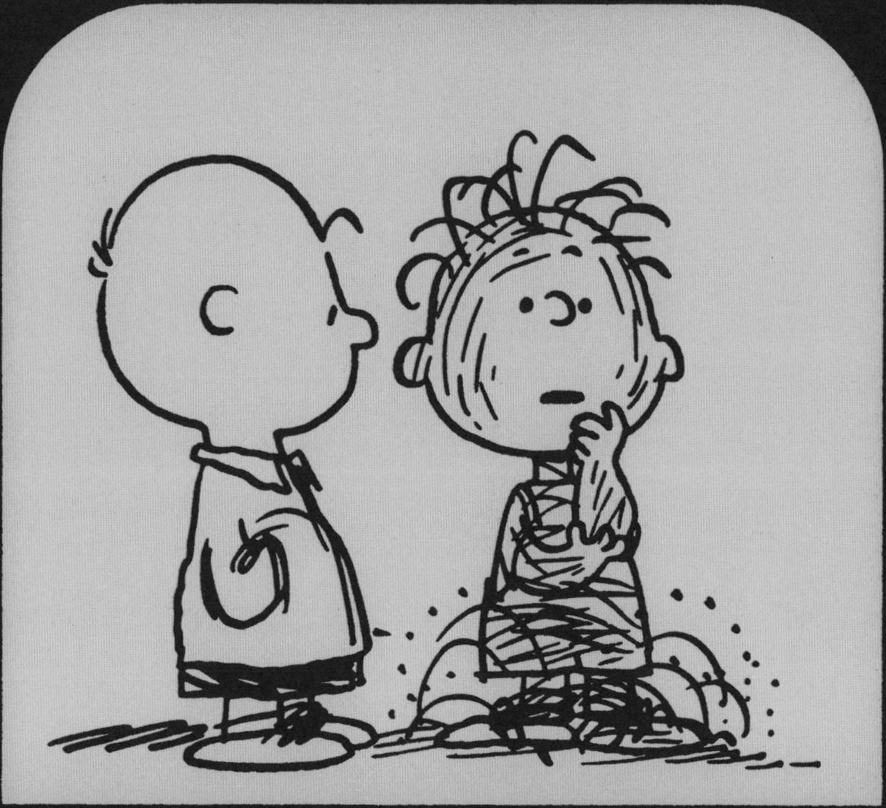

"You know what I think a friend is, Charlie Brown?"

"A friend is someone who accepts you for what you are."

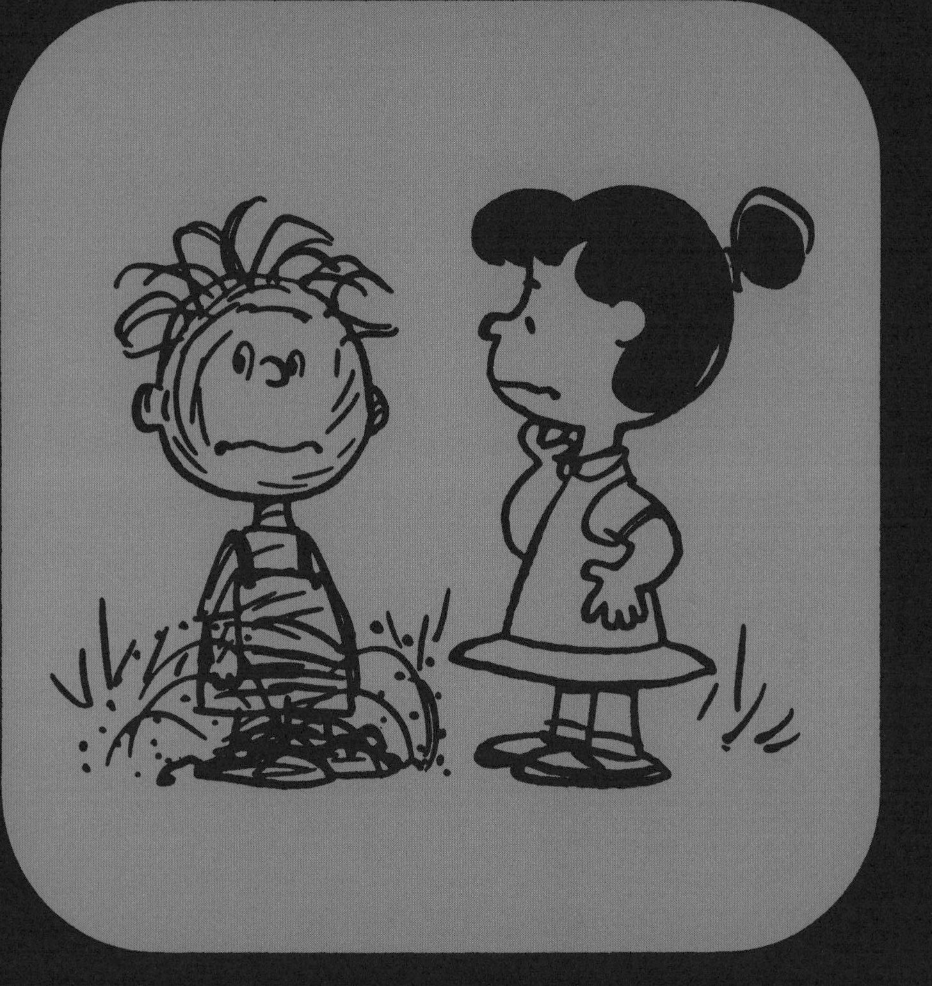

"A friend
is someone
who is not jealous
if you have
other friends."

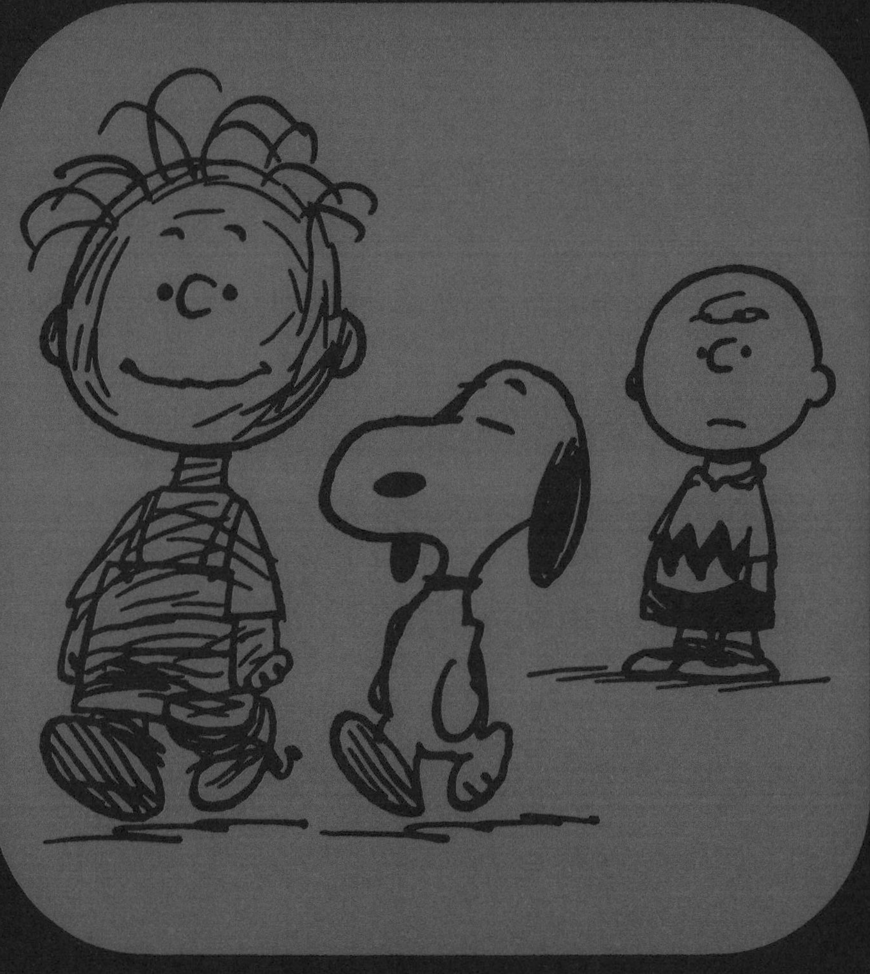

"A friend is someone you have things in common with, Charlie Brown."

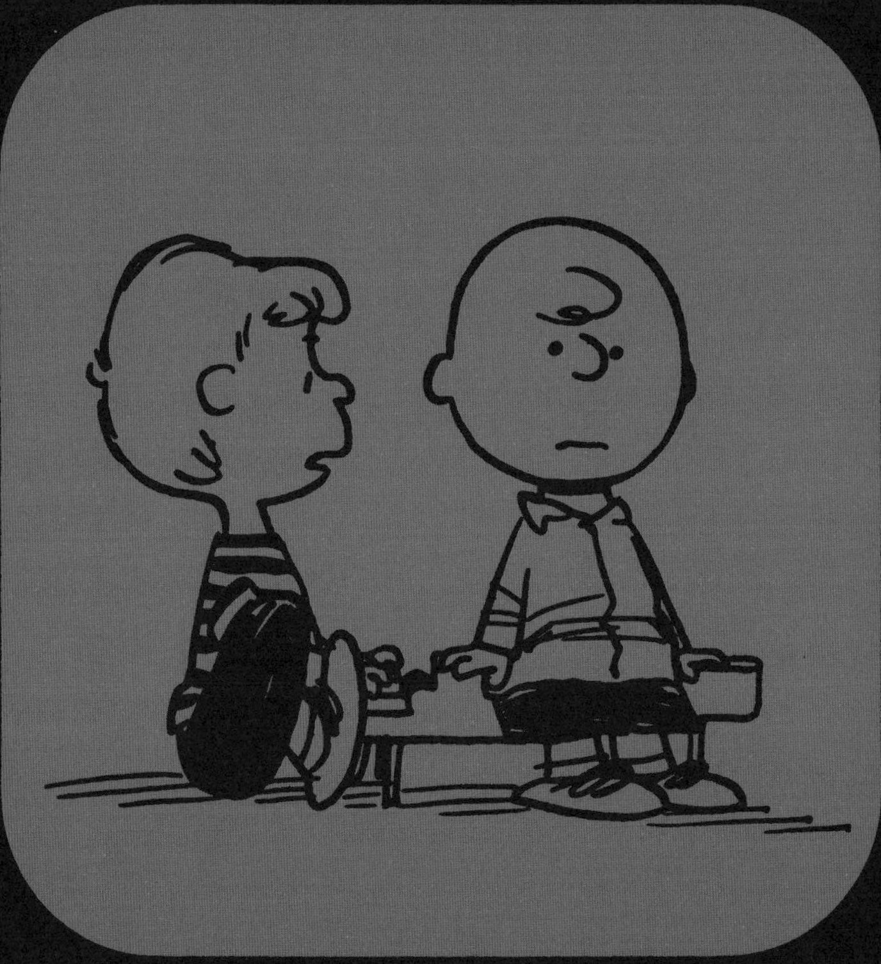

"A friend
is someone
who understands
why you like your
strawberry sodas
without any
strawberries
in them."

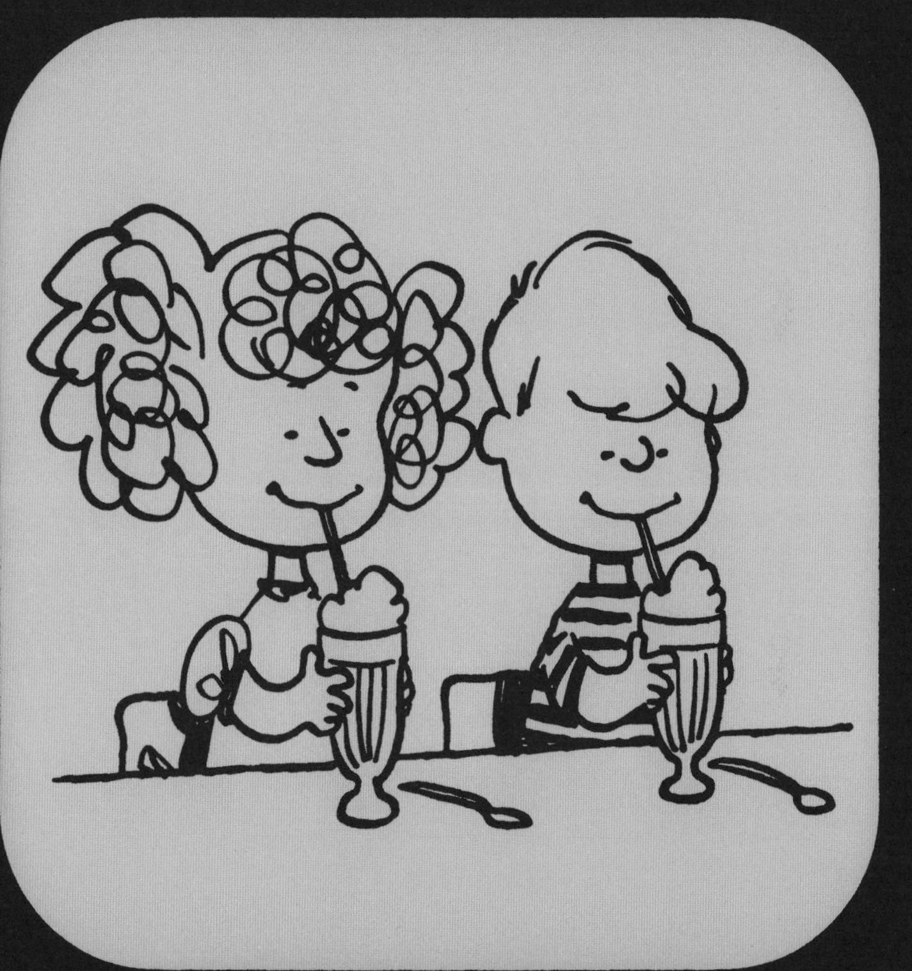

"A friend
is someone
who doesn't think
it's crazy to collect
old Henry Busse
records!"

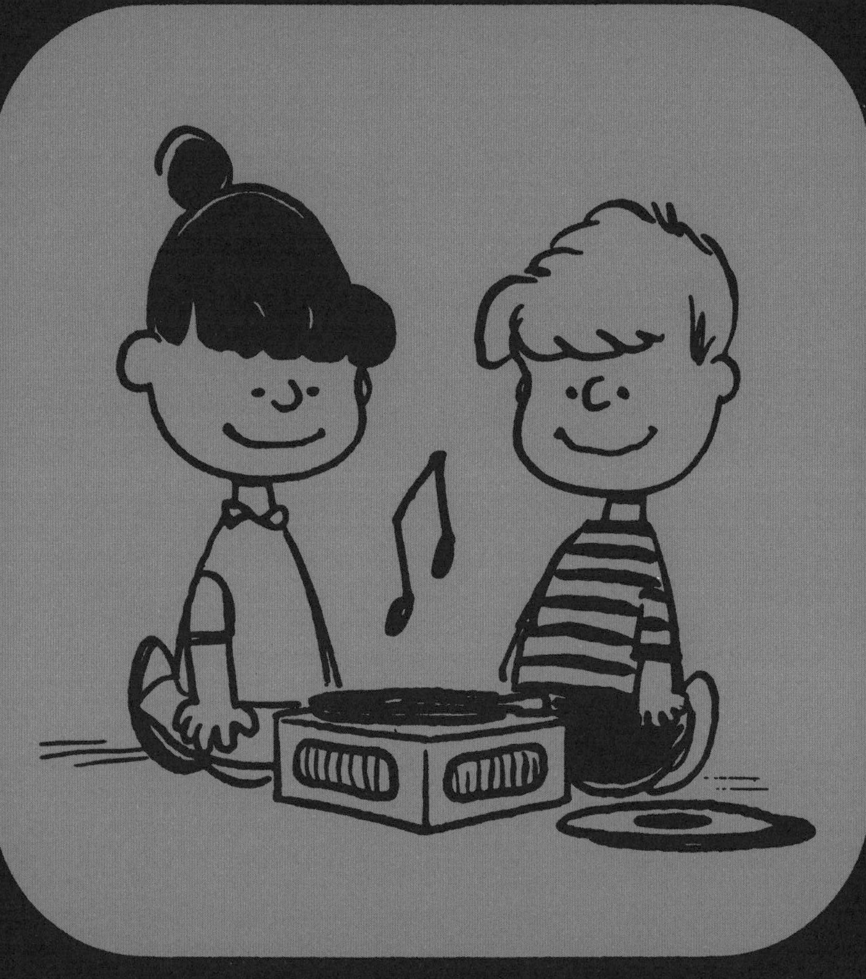

"A friend is someone who likes the same music you like."

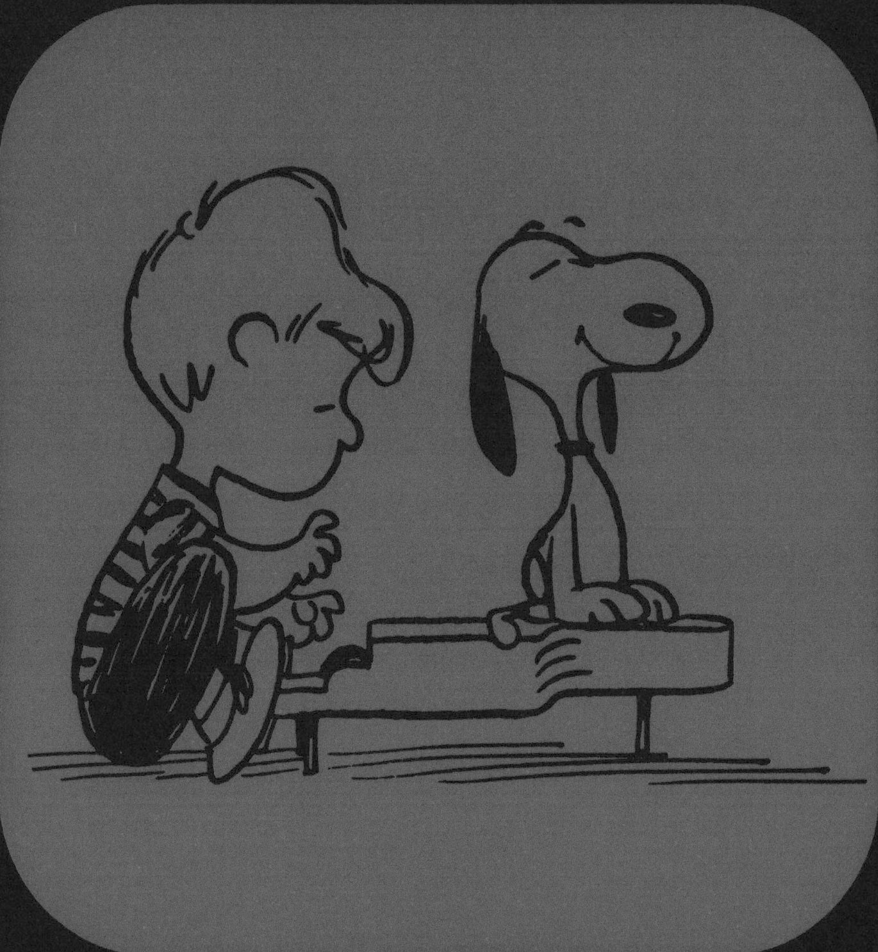

"A friend
is someone
who can't stand
the same sort of
music you can't
stand!"

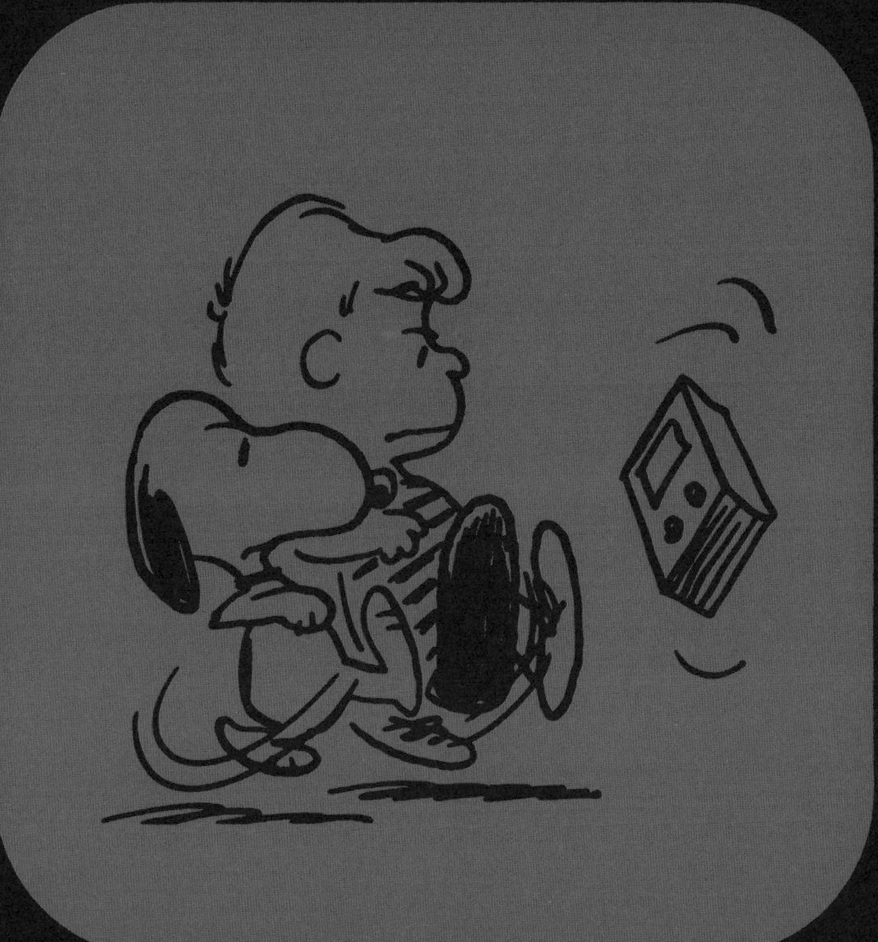

"A friend is someone who will hold a place in line for you."

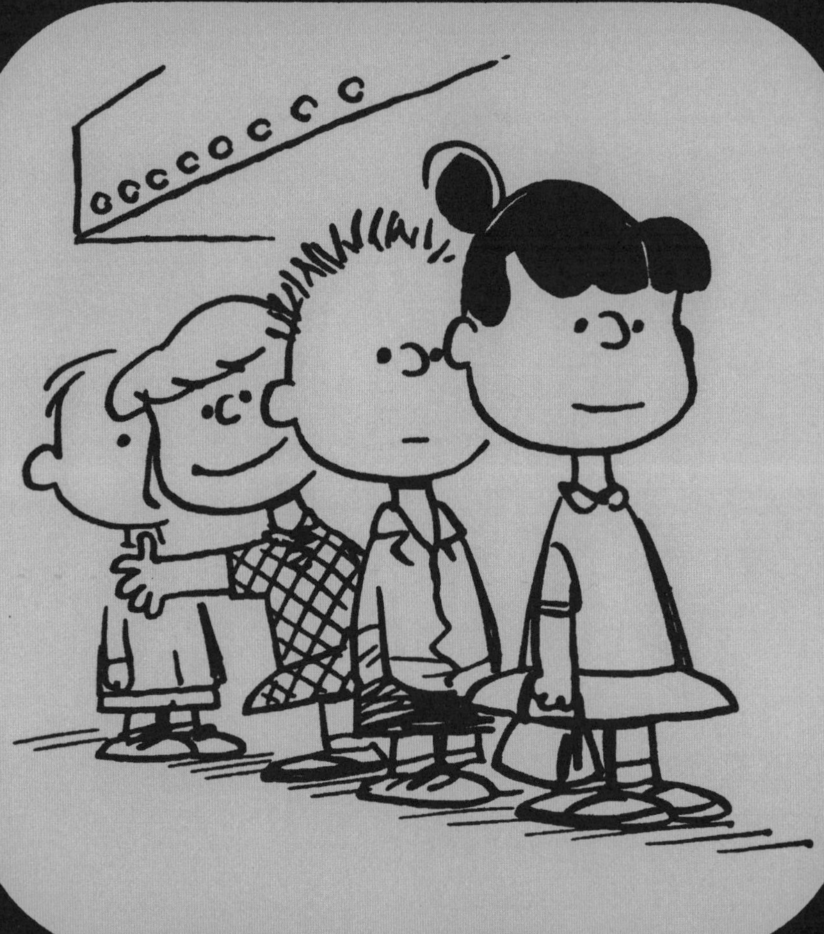

"A friend
is someone who
sticks up for you
when you're
not there."

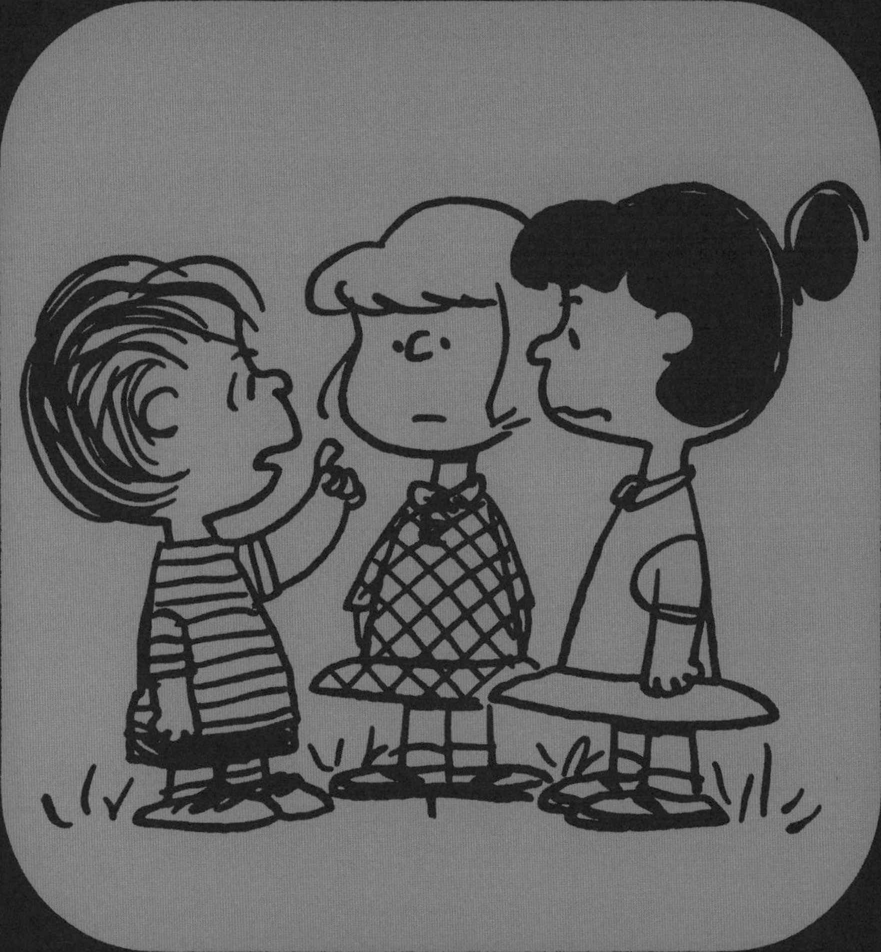

"A friend is someone who sends you a postcard when he's on vacation."

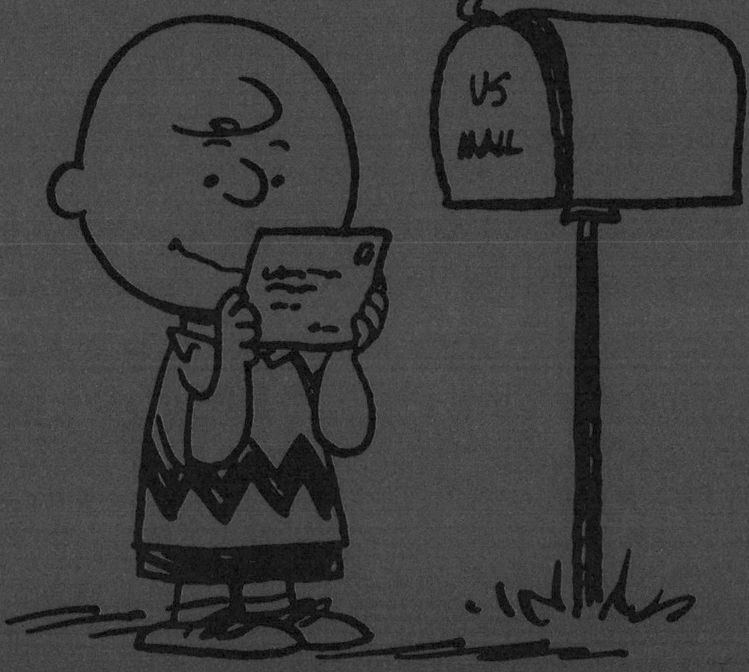
US MAIL

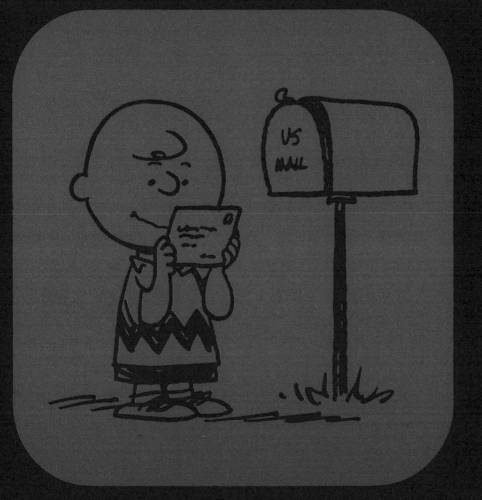

"A friend is someone who doesn't criticize something you just bought."

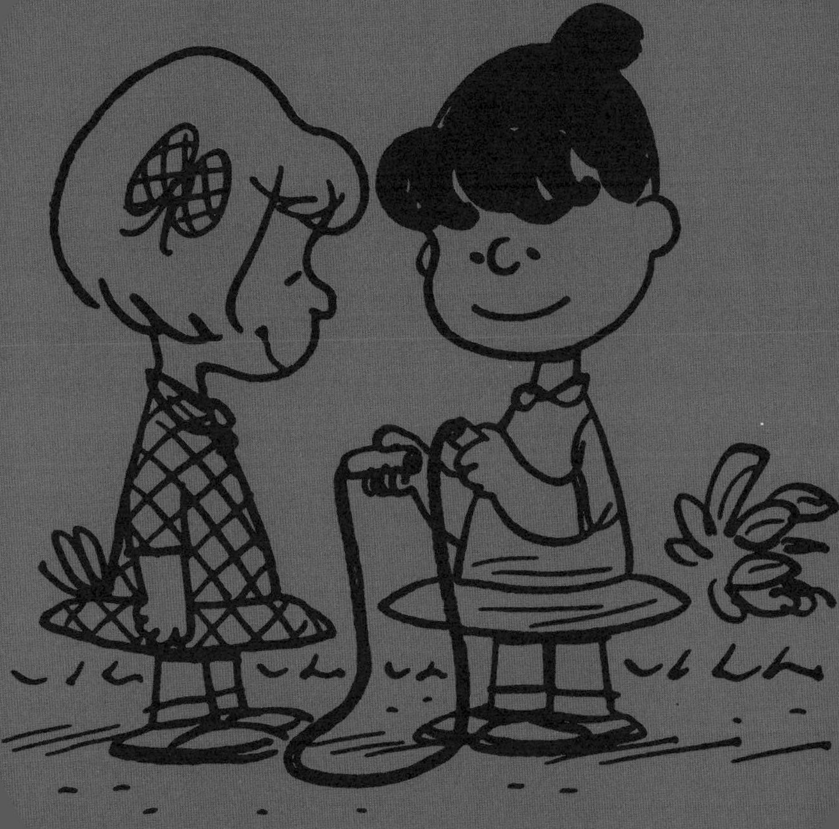

"A friend is someone who takes off the leash!"

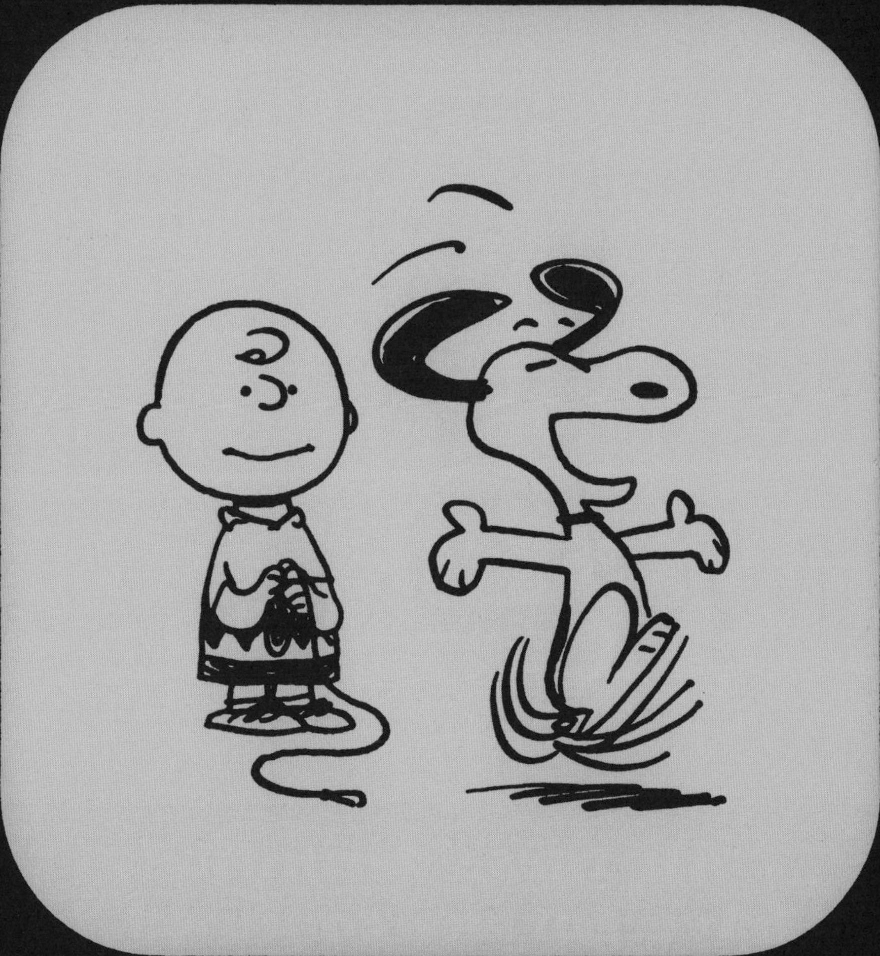

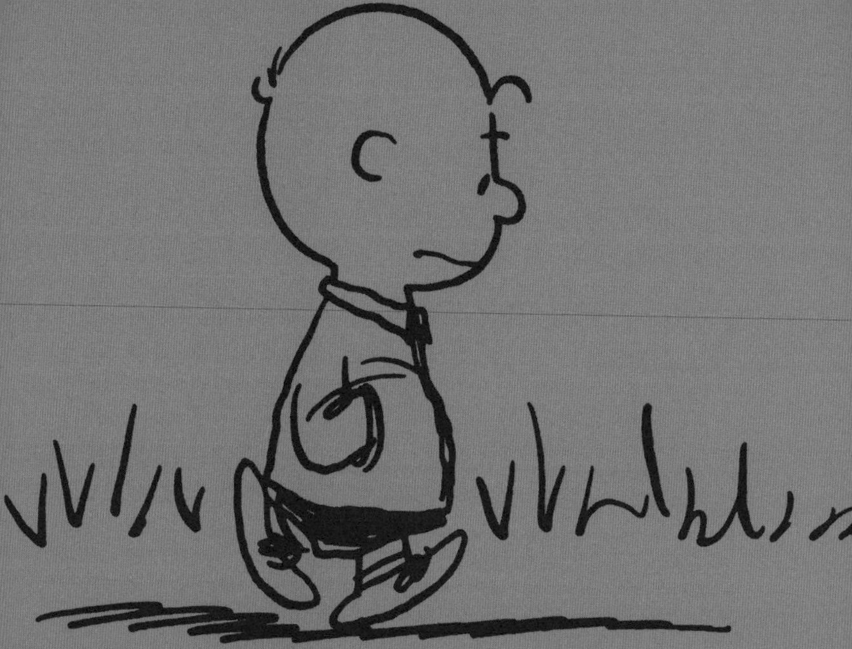

"All these definitions have got me confused."

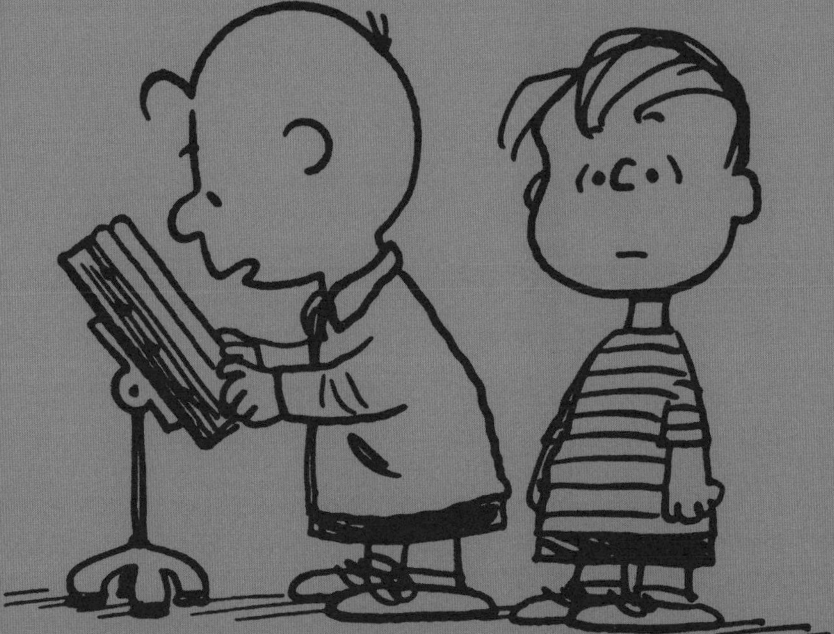

"'Friend . . . A person whom one knows well, and is fond of.'"

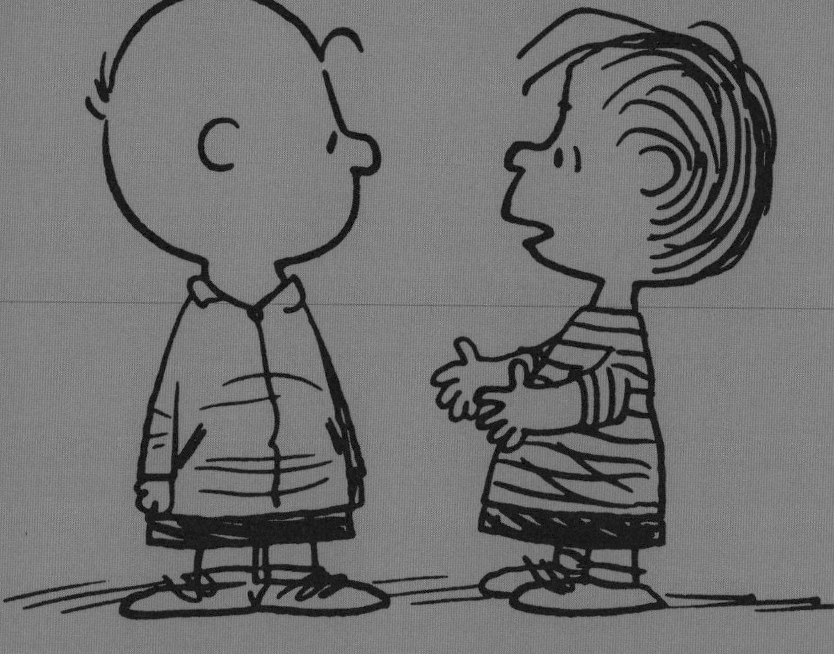

"That's me!"

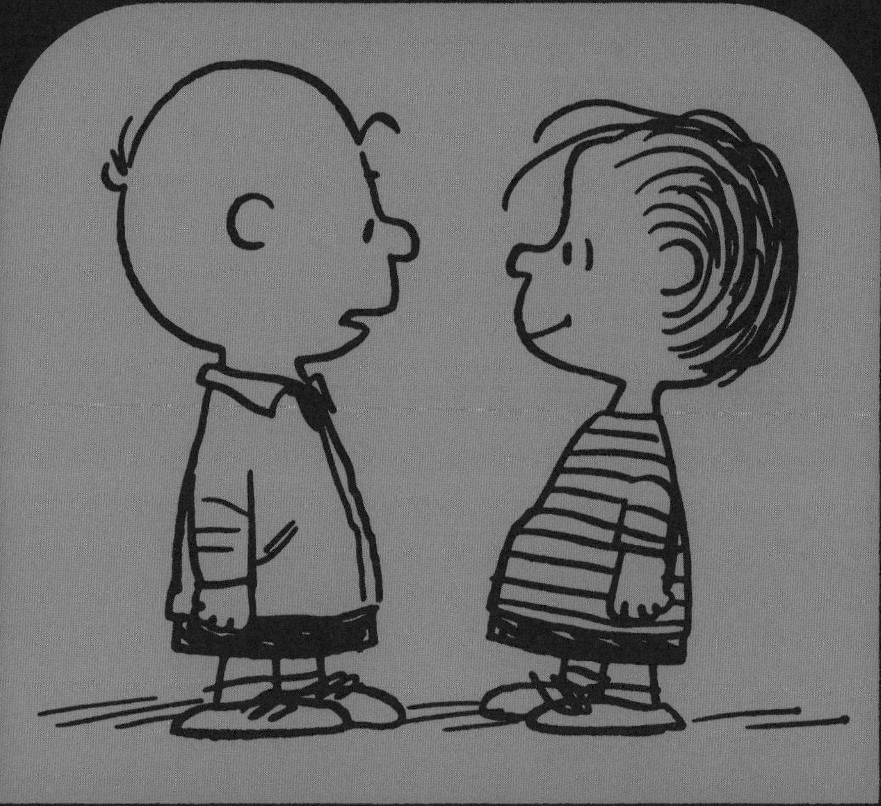

"What?"

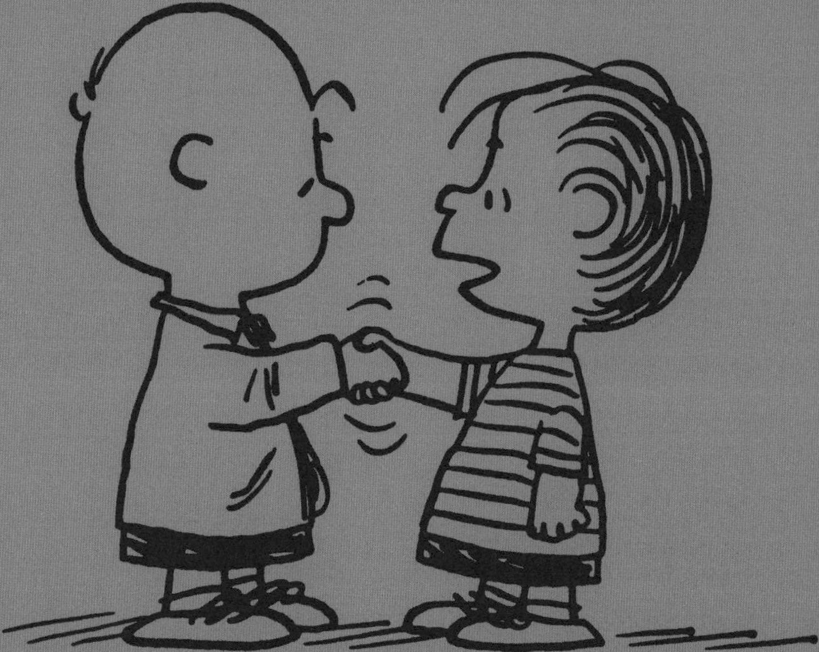

“I said, ‘That’s me!’
I’m your friend, Charlie Brown!’”

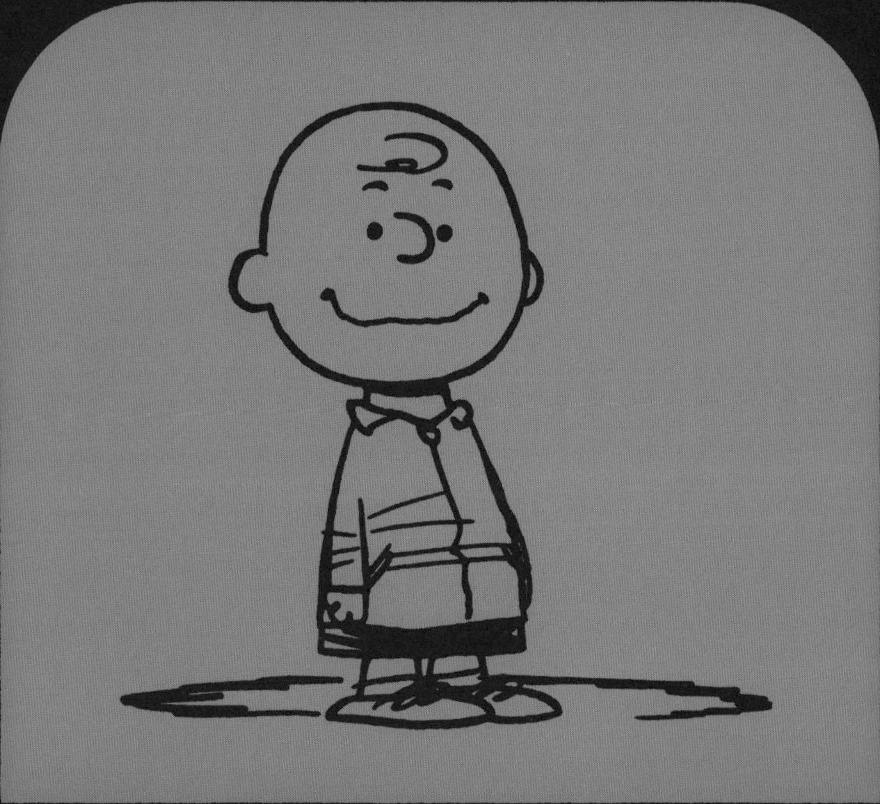

"Well, what do you know?"